STANDING BEFORE THE UNKNOWN

poems by

Howard Joel Schechter

dedicated to

Robert Schechter, my dear brother,

who, of all my creative adventures, likes my poetry best

laughing water press

imagine

imagine,
the mind
a line

each idea
a board
with a zipper on

each tooth
a different color

put them all together
stuff them into a leather pouch

hang it on the wall

blow it up!
explode it!

that
is understanding

<u>anyway</u>

i live
i die

tomorrow
they serve pancakes
at the Parkside

anyway

<u>flow</u>

flow
slow
into
the very
ordinary

<u>pom</u>

and the japanese man said
"isn't Love
a Western idea?"

<u>moment</u>

a butterfly
buzzes
the megalithic stone circles
4000 years bold

they play pub music
in dublin
every wednesday night

south dakota
freezes early
this year

on the same night
we walk the beach

in california

shirtless
to a three quarter moon

enuf

it's enuf
to be dry
and listen
to the rain

drop

sense

a good friend died yesterday

today
another had a baby

tomorrow my daughter gets married

so
how do you make sense of that?

<u>his teaching</u>
(for dr. shankar)

non attachment to what is
non-attachment to what is not

non-rejection of what is
non-rejection of what is not

acceptance
equals
quiet mind

awareness only

breathing in

it's only the out-breath
that matters

<u>sweet face girl</u>
            (for Barbara Lee)

big hearted woman
tender woman

gentle loving
nurturing
and kind

life giving

forged by years
and tears
of children

body
the fragrance of rose

delicious mouth

her mystery
a cup of honey

feeling the pain
of the earth
and the ache
of it's people

sustaining those in close

free
from most
conditioned thought

sweet face girl
i love you

<u>to my teacher harry sloan, on retiring from leading workshops</u>

once upon a time
there was harry

he taught me how to help
heal
the emotional wounds
we all suffer

birthing a rush
into the present

thank you harry
for the teaching

it has been a joy
a blessing
a blossoming
for me
to do this work

but now
no more heavy lifting

light and
lighter

from here
on
in

(November, 2006, at Esalen upon deciding to hang it up)

<u>writing</u>

nothing to say

just fingers on letters
tapping on keys

words appearing
out of the ethers
out of the Mystery

no - thing

 the lightness of
creating

the heaviness of it
too

on a journey
with the home team

while
i'm learning
about fear

my fear
which thrives
as i push it away

which fades
as i allow it

fear is real
but it is not

Who We Are

<u>Alan Seal died today</u>

Alan Seal died today
and it makes me sad

He was the reason my mother wouldn't let me play football

Alan played
for Central
and got his leg broken
by a guy from Northeastern

The bone stuck out
real ugly
it got infected
and my mother came to know

Then
she wouldn't let me play
for Mumford
("Live and die, for Samuel Mumford High")

I was crushed

Coach Kelley recruited me
he wanted a smart Jewish kid at quarterback

Alan Seal died today
making the passage of Time
and this fleeting Life
so clear

all else
confused

the only clarity
knowing
it's all a Mystery   (continued)

and i
can never
ever
understand it

dipsea trail nail

on the mt. tamalpais dipsea trail
in a step on the steep
there's a nail

poorly pounded
folded over
squashed

now
seventy years later
i see that ugly nail
every time I climb

and think
sloppy work
does not work
here

i can feel into that hammer holder's head
 "oh shit
i bent the nail
should i pull it?
should i leave it?"

i wish he 'd made a different choice

i wish i'd made some different choices
too

Uganda House

driving
in crowded london
i notice a flash
in the corner of my eye

i turn
i see
Uganda House

memories flooding through

30 years ago
wandering these streets
tired and lost
looking for this place
with my friend marilyn

preparing our trip to Africa
just invented
on a napkin
in a veggie restaurant
soho, london, england

at Uganda House
a giant black man
fixed on my long hippie hair
eyed me
grilled me
relented
gave the visas

then
arab air
to Nairobi

(continued)

"hired" a car
bought tents
3 month safari
camping adventure

every night
huge fires
to keep the lions
away

false protection
of canvas

leaving Uganda
the day idi amin
hitler of the place
celebrated his first year

on the road to mombassa
i flipped the peugeot
and the Kenya police
were silly

taking measurements
from the end of the skid mark
to their left elbow

on the coast
recuperating
i met andrea

we came home
and married

i california carpentered
until our daughter
michelle
was born

then
took a job
bought a house

dug in

now
in my studio
i look at a photo of my dear dead friend david
marilyn
and i

long hair and beards
floating
near the headwaters of the nile

skinny
skinny
skinny

all we ate was boiled cabbage

the trumpet call of elephants
rhinos busting to the surface

beautiful
ugly
and dangerous

now
way
way downstream
I kiss my wife
barbara

I see michelle
a grown woman

(continued)

and marry andrea
to her new husband
rick

dear 'Sbergie

"dear 'Sbergie,
 thank you for the days we spent together...."

how you love that rock and roll

having fun
with your wife marilyn
and friends

travelling
children
dogs
cats
a good
bad book
a bad
good movie

i remember our trip to Scotland
and how we argued over change
at the gas station
because we hadn't cleared the air
about something else

then we did

and quickly
we fell back in love

we walked in the rain
and saw castles
and ate huge fatty breakfasts
whenever possible

i'm sorry we didn't take that trip to India
we had always talked about

i treasure our times
living together
our commune
two couples
in the suburbs

we walked together a lot
around the crater in Kenya
down the "county not maintained"
"in walnut creek

the last time i saw you
in the presence of great green mother ocean waves

where time passed gloriously
with pete
the sweet
we walked and talked and swam

you looked frail
in your white under shorts bathing suit

did you still have that little pony tail?

i felt for you a loving protectiveness
like a father to a son   (continued)

then
again
sometimes
you were
a father to me

you dove fearlessly into biting cold water
then
you were anything but frail

in Africa
you taught me to swim
with a love for the wet

in the middle of nowhere
you jumped into a lake
infested with killer bacteria
and they never touched you
i think they mistook you for a fish

for all the pain of your recoveries
and your devotion
to your healing
to marilyn's healing
i am amazed

in awe
at your incredible persistence
and profound courage

in your presence
i felt accepted
just as i am

so loved
not judged
just loved

that's all

with you
i could
relax

be my best Self

as barbara says, "your eyes open deep into your soul"
to a vast treasure of kindness

gentleness
and caring

when richie phoned me
that day
and told me you died
it was a gun blast
to the belly

my head jerked back
my brain went empty
everything went blurrrrrr

i was immobile
and unable
to grasp

i jumped on the bike
to ride into the air
alone

there you gave me another gift

my senses
and awareness
hyper-keen

refined
heightened to full receptivity
(continued)

raptured by the yellow green hills
and the white mist

and the laughter of children

when my mind jumped from
allowing and accepting
to thinking
i moved from fresh air
to a hall of twisted mirrors

filled with limitation
and confusion

then
i let go

and rode that bike
deep breathing

embracing the all
and the everything

the smoky smell of dinner barbecues

friends gathering
people chattering

a little boy riding a one wheeler

i was perfectly free

in a state of grace
i knew it was okay
because you showed me

it is a moving
not an ending

there is no ending

just constant
unfathomable
change

Horodok: A Visit to My Father's Birth Village in Belarus

They said,
"There's nothing left."

What they mean is,
"There is nothing Jewish left."

There is today
A lively village
Sweet with houses
Streets
Yards
And a river running through it

A beautiful
Lovely river
The only thing in that place
My father spoke of fondly

I stood on the bridge
With my brother Neal
And watched

In my mind's eye I saw a little Jewish boy
Face full of love
Running
Cracking stick against trees

1912   (continued)

I smiled
Complete
Having danced with my father's river

The streets are paved now
Not mud anymore

The houses are floored now
Not dirt anymore

A town square
A statue of Lenin
A bird crapping on the visionary's head

Smiling peasants
Mouths full of metal
Soviet era dentistry

Babushkas everywhere

Donkey carts
Laden with hay
Women on top
Sleeping away

A gracious old couple
Helped us
With guidance
And blessings
From their Catholic God

People
We had learned to hate
For their happy complicity with the slaughter of Jews

Their children
Now proving kind

An occasional disagreeable look
Disdain or fear
Jews from America
Might mean change

An old woman
From her dying bed
Invites us in

Orphaned
Adopted by a Jewish family

In her modest cottage
She hypnotizes us with stories
Of life
And love
In Horodok

Then she breaks weeping
Remembering her family
Forced into the street
Marched to the killing fields

She muttered the names
All twelve
Hershel and Esther
Dovid and Wolf
Perished with the five thousand that day

Outside the town
On a desperate knoll
Killed like cattle

Falling into pits
Like pigs

Onto the next village the Nazi murders went   (continued)

Slaughtering more '
Another Jewish village
Another killing field

The vicious butchery
Over and over and over
Again

Screaming
Or quiet
They prayed
And died
For the crime of being Jewish

"Yea, though I walk through the valley of the shadow of death
I fear no evil
For thou art with me......"

The entire countryside of the Pale
mass graves under foot

We honored the dead
With prayers of remembrance
At the memorial for Horodok

Next to the rust colored
Marble
Faded blue obelisk
We stood
And chanted our prayers

Asher in tallis
Leading the circle
Singing our grief

and Rage

Seething at the evil
Who called itself Man

On leaving
Our bus was stuck
Reminding us
That earth is master

Rejoice in gratitude
For the beauty
That has become our lives

For our parents' courage
To leave that finished place
And bequeath us freedom

An old man
Veteran of the red army
Did us Jewish geography

He showed us Schneider's old house
And Kauffman's
And Resnick's the butcher

Children play now
In the overgrown lot
That was the synagogue

We wandered the streets
Giving sweets
To the kids

There are no Jews in Horodok
Just us

Reality

the red egg of Reality
immersed
above and below
the plane of illusion

a cottage

we lived
in a converted garage
with a loft
and a lot
of love

blue english dishes
and my paintings
on the wall

a cottage
where we lived
and worked
and played
as the sea broke wild
with wonder
through windows
in the front

where andrea was ill
and recovered

where michelle was born

where i learned
to pray

the birth

when she was born
in the instant she arrived
i knew her
profoundly
from Before

forever
i have known her

blessings

michelle

when you look at me
with eyes full of love

and smile

everything
bursts inside

i kneel
to kiss you
and thank God
for our blessings

first poem for michelle

i held her in my arms
when she couldn't sleep
in the morning
five weeks old

i walked the room
in an old blue t-shirt
and red boxer shorts
until she calmed

we fell
into bed
michelle
on my chest

tiny
half asleep

within minutes
she slipped
deeper
to my side

sleeping in the nook of my shoulder
like a grown woman

a moment between sleepings
awoke me

i looked into her eyes
and cried

11 months

now
when we play
it's not papa and baby
it's papa and somebody
Real

before
it was wonderful

precious
and warm

now
it's better
unique
and exciting

expressing
herself

now
behind the infant
there is really Somebody there

out

i went out
with michelle
to see a friend
and have dinner

our first time "out"
just father and daughter
papa and little girl   (continued)

she sat tall
and i was full

she sat tall
and joy
overwhelmed me

argentina dawn

out for a walk
before mama awakes
pushing the carriage
around the square
early in the morning

we stop for a coffee
corner café
café con leche
warm bun for the little girl

she eats slow
i drink fast

because little girls
get restless

we circle
the square
twice
before dawn
wakes up
buenos aires

a reminder

my daughter
at my wife's breast
looks into my eyes
and smiles

grounding me
in the Present

reminding me
that life
lives
itself

seeing my daughter seeing herself

a california tahoe weekend
in a rented wooded cottage

reminds me of other weekends
in michigan cottages
where the street ended at the lake
and the smell
was perfectly
wet

and i wonder
what smells
will she remember

Completely
===

a little girl sleeps

tiny fingers
tiny curls

and i'm filled with wonder
deeply touched

don't the people who start wars
have children
who sleep perfectly
too

or do they miss it
Completely

"right dad?"
===

we were ready to sleep
talking about what to do tomorrow
and michelle said,

"we're lucky dad
because there's always tomorrow"

"and tomorrow
and tomorrow
and tomorrow after that"

"tomorrow
forever."
"right dad?"

my daughter 16 years old in her mother's wedding dress

my daughter
in her mother's wedding dress

standing in front of the house
i saw her
from afar

shining and beautiful

fresh
alive
strong

i was moved
for the years
and their passing

she was a child
now a woman

i was a boy
now a man

the joy and the sorrow
the years and the tears
all that was
and all that will be...

my daughter
in her mother's wedding dress

two poems by michelle, age 8

feathers

feathers are beautiful
and stars are nice to me

from michelles' homework

as foolish as lying to a friend
as sweet as lemon maraing pie
as strong as Willy punching you
as angry as my mom if i took drugs
as steady as a big statchyou
as nervous as singing on stage
as useful as a chock board
as old as a new born baby
as easy as trying to not watch tv

Ganga Ma

praying in it
playing in it

brushing teeth in it

dying in it

mother Ganges
Ganga Ma

The Source

We fuss on the surface
we fight
we make war
over issues

but really, there are no issues
there is only Knowing
and Forgetting

we are Divine Spirits
God in body form

destined to flower
and fruit
and decay

so,
when nations are at war
or people fight
do not believe the
"blah
blah
blah"

or, "he said, she said,
"blah
blah
blah"

No, it's not about reasons
it's about Ignorance
or Forgetting

Nothing more!

natural man

non-denial of what is

clean
and
simple

painful too

no one is owned
no one is owning

everything is connected

honestly
courageously
free

there is still hope

I was studying Spanish
listening to Mexican radio
when Bishop Carlos said

"the more materialistic the society
the more the people hunger for God."

<u>running</u>

changing time

moment to movement
movement to moment

hard
easy

pleasure
pain

the difficult parts are best taken lightly

<u>at wood valley, big island, hawaii</u>

sitting on the Temple floor
it came clear

what we call "real"
is Illusion

what we call "illusion"
is Real

the Real world
is an empty room

open and uncluttered

the wind blows through it

Illusion
is a room filled with over-stuffed chairs

in the emptiness
the truth is clear

freedom is natural

and happiness
is Real

<u>at whittington beach, big island, hawaii</u>

standing on the shore
white waves pounding

unflinching rock

vast mother ocean
focusing into drops

we too
are the Vastness

focused into Being
infinitely One

The 'Cane That Fucked Hawaii

like a monster plant
rolling on sixteen wheels

the sugar cane truck

stalks of harvest
hangin' over
tentacles flopping everywhere

The Cane That Fucked Hawaii

so valuable
they stole the Islands for it

now
one hundred years later
Sovereignty is the cry

and nobody is listening

nobody who owns cane fields
or pineapple plantations

hotels
resorts
shipyards
or golf courses

colonize a people
and forgiveness doesn't come easy

but the old folks do i
they are beyond anger
into the wisdom
and the kindness of Aloha

(continued)

warm smiles
beautiful faces
the Spirit of Shared Breath

<u>a commentary on the movies</u>

why so much violence in the movies?

because
as a culture
we are resistant to the Sacred

we have forgotten the obvious Truth
indigenous peoples have known
since the Beginning

there is a Mystery
and it is sacred
beyond understanding

call it God
or chopped liver
we need the fullness of Spirit

Spirit unites the Cosmos

most of us Know
though it's often hidden
that there is a Power greater than us
that science will never name

to base a society
on materialism alone is foolish

like trying to breath
in a vacuum

denying the obvious truth
we gorge on over-stimulation
the Red eyed Monster
hoping to fill the hole

constantly seeking satisfaction
never satisfied

violence is the symptom
Emptiness the cause

open window

I sit up
in her bed
musing

the sounds and smells of Nature
drift through the open window

they lull me
they fill me
they rock me
to Bliss

<u>beef and barley soup at the deli</u>

before he died
my dad visited at the beach

we were together
everyday

when i worked
he read

while i painted
he sat

when i drove
he snoozed

no matter what else was going on
we ate lunch together

beef and barley soup
at the deli

one day he took a bath
and asked me to help

in that moment
i knew
he was offering me the chance
to repay him
for Everything

there is no bullshit in death

in trance
i walked across the snow-whitened grass
kicking clods of cold turf

moments before
my mother was dead
lying face up
in her hospital bed

i dropped to my knees
on the antiseptic floor
without thought

i prayed through tears
as in an ancient ritual
learned
but unknown

i cried
and gushed my gratitude
for a mother who knew how to love

it was deeply sad
but strangely okay

there is no bullshit in death

once

maria
the italian girl
with deep-brown eyes
and a plain beautiful face

she haunts me with adventure
romantic nights
mysterious days

paris
rome
milan

moving the world
stopping here
stopping there
not stopping anywhere

i would like to know you
maria

who was your father?
your first lover?
where exactly is milan?

14th Avenue

a young girl
with penetrating eyes
stands by the bus stop
waiting

seducing traffic

hoping for the man
who will steal her boredom
and make everything
All Right

social movements

the fate of social movements
is to degenerate into fashion

affectation

affectation
makes beautiful women ugly

smart men stupid

and everybody
Less

meditating on the sound of the ocean

the difficult part is in
between

the crash is easy

soundlessness
is the challenge

meditation

meditation is a mind shower
and milk
at the breast of the Goddess

It's All True

the little boy
in a coffee shop
with his mother

sits on a high backed stool
sipping cocoa
with joy

his mouth bubbles foam

tiny droplets of milk
caught on his lips
reaching toward the sky

he beams in an ecstasy of taste

closes his eyes
digging deep
into the warm soft bun
clutched savagely in tiny hands

he looks at me
in glee
and i feel the sweetness of his youth

as i drive back
the splattered skunk
bleeds helplessly on the road

san quentin prison on my left
broadcasts it's pain

the boy
the squirrel
the prison   (continued)

the joy
the death
the pain

it's all True

<u>sons of freedom</u>

during the War
my war
our war
Vietnam

my constant hope
was that it would end
RIGHT FUCKING NOW!

i remember thinking
"if i had a magic wand
i would wave it
and end this horrible farce"

i marched
i wrote
i argued

i cursed the cops in ugly jump suits

i agonized and suffered
with the suffering

i screamed into the empty night

"i won't go
to fight that piece of shit"

i was a draft dodger
with a legal hustle

still i felt guilty
for the guys who went
sucking swamp
getting their balls blown off

in spite of my certainty
there was always doubt
was i just afraid?

"real men" are brave
they fight wars
and spit in the face of death

i respected
even admired
those who fought

i thought
they had conquered their fear
and i was still stuck with mine

but "No," say the vets
"it 's not courage
it's not conquering
it's blind obedience
and a touch of stupidity"

"you're young
you don't know
you think you have no choice"

"you go
you fight
you do what they say
you just do it"   (continued)

the presence of horror
did not build courage
it sometimes broke it

fear locked deep into the bones
anger to drag around for a lifetime

sometimes it slips out
when your wife grabs you lovingly from behind
or a helicopter passes over head

when it's real dark
and you can't hear a thing

it is time
for those who fought in Vietnam
and those who fought against it
to come Home together
for Peace
and celebrate our brotherhood

because we are all
Sons of Freedom

<u>stinson song</u>

It'n the mountain that separates
The city from the sea
The mountain that separates
The heaviness from me

It's the mountain that separates
The tranquil from the mad
It's the mountain that separates
The freshness from the fad

It's the mountain that separates
The city from the sea
It's the mountain that separates
Futurama from me

Made in the USA
Charleston, SC
11 February 2013